My Sense of
TOUCH

Ellen Lawrence

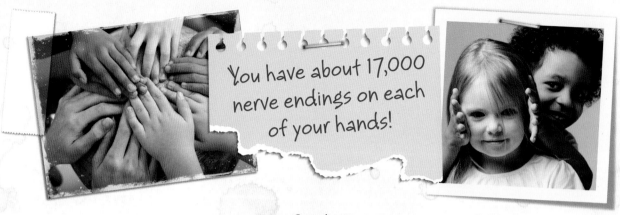

You have about 17,000 nerve endings on each of your hands!

Consultant:
Suzy Gazlay, MA
Recipient, Presidential Award for Excellence in Science Teaching

Photography © Shutterstock 2023 ADragan; Aleks Melnik; Alsu; Anna-Mari West; antoniodiaz; Astarina; Brent Hofacker; Digital Images Studio; Dmitry Lobanov; DmitryStock; Drawlab19; Eldi D; Elena Pimukova; EniaKlever; greenland; Gwens Graphic Studio; HardtIllustrations; HelenField; Howard Klaaste; iofoto; John T Takai; JPRFPhotos; Katflare; Krakenimages.com; LintangDesign; Melianiaka Kanstantsin; Melica; MIA Studio; Michael C. Gray; michaeljung; Michelle D. Milliman; mijatmijatovic; Monkey Business Images; Natalia van D; Nik Merkulov; PedroNevesDesign; PenWin; PictuLandra; prochasson frederic; Redcollegiya; Roman Malyshev; RTimages; Ryan DeBerardinis; SciePro; serazetdinov; Sergio33; Simple Line; sirtravelalot; suerz; sumkinn; Tartila; Valentyn Volkov; vesilvio; WEExp; WilleeCole Photography; WINS86; XiXinXing
Additional photography provided by Ruby Tuesday Books: Science Artwork/SPL/Science Photo/SuperStock (p. 7); Ruby Tuesday Books (p. 9); Shutterstock/Ruby Tuesday Books (pp. 10-11); Burger/Phanie/SuperStock (p. 14); Shutterstock (p. 18)

Published by Sequoia Kids Media,
an imprint of Sequoia Publishing & Media, LLC

Sequoia Publishing & Media, LLC,
a division of Phoenix International Publications, Inc.

8501 West Higgins Road
Chicago, Illinois 60631

© 2024 Sequoia Publishing & Media, LLC
First published © Ruby Tuesday Books Limited

CustomerService@PhoenixInternational.com

You're so SOFT!

I read with my hands!

www.SequoiaKidsMedia.com

Library of Congress Control Number: 2023935238

ISBN: 979-8-7654-0301-3

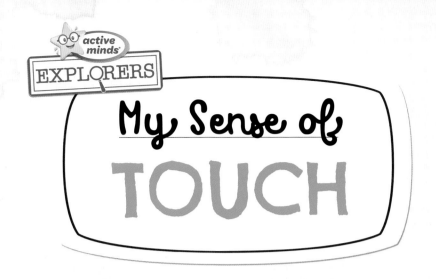

active minds EXPLORERS

My Sense of TOUCH

Table of Contents

Words shown in **bold** in the text are explained in the glossary.

It's HOT!

Your Sense of Touch

So soft!

Ouch! That cactus plant is very prickly. Mmmmmm. This puppy's fur is so soft.

Every day, your **sense** of touch brings you hundreds of different touch **sensations**.

OUCH!

If you accidentally place your hand on something hot or sharp, you feel pain.

The pain is your body's way of keeping you safe by telling you to stop touching now!

ROUGH!

From the tip of your nose to the bottom of your feet, your body can feel the world around it.

Just how does your sense of touch work, though? Let's check it out.

HOT!

SHARP!

COLD!

Your body has five senses, which are seeing, hearing, smelling, tasting, and touching. Your senses help you enjoy your world and help keep you safe.

5

Your Skin Up Close

The part of your body that lets you feel the world around you is your skin.

Your skin is made up of three layers.

The outside layer, which you can see, is called the **epidermis**.

Your epidermis is made of tiny **cells** called skin cells.

Inside your epidermis, new skin cells are growing all the time.

That's good news, because about 40,000 old, dead skin cells fall off your body every minute!

Goodbye old skin cells!

Some of the cells in your epidermis make a substance called **melanin**. It's melanin that gives your skin its color. People with dark skin have more melanin in their skin than people with pale skin.

Your sense of touch is spread throughout every bit of your skin.

Skin cells

This photo was created by a **microscope**. It shows the cells in the top layer of a person's skin.

7

Meet Your Touching Cells

Beneath your outer layer of skin is a second layer called the **dermis**.

This part of your skin is home to cells called **nerve endings**.

These cells are sometimes also called touch sensors or touch receptors.

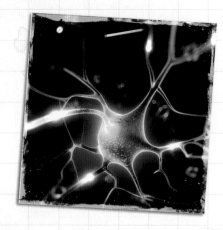

Touch your nose with your finger. Do you feel your finger gently pressing on your nose? Can you feel how the tip of your nose is wobbly? You feel these things because there are nerve endings in both your nose and finger.

All over your body, your skin contains nerve endings.

It's the job of your nerve endings to **detect** all the different sensations you feel through your skin.

This picture shows what the three layers of your skin look like.

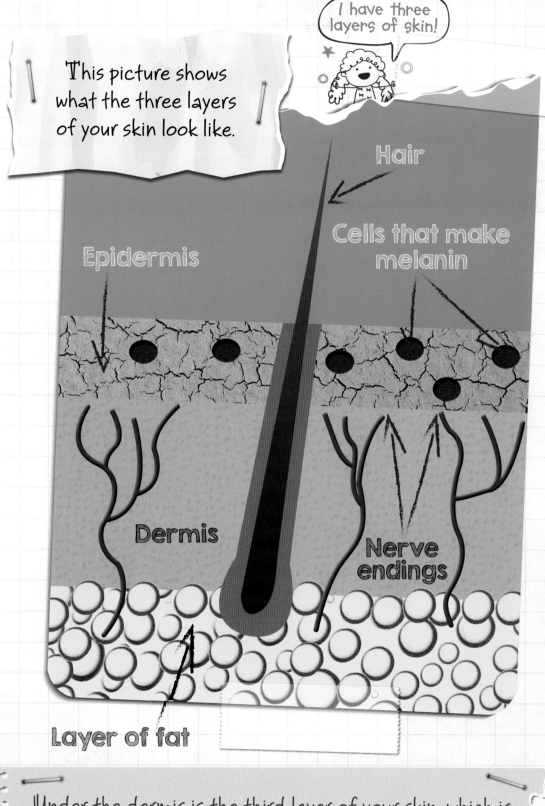

I have three layers of skin!

Hair

Epidermis

Cells that make melanin

Dermis

Nerve endings

Layer of fat

Under the dermis is the third layer of your skin, which is made of squishy fat. This fat helps keep your body warm and protects your insides if you bump into something. Hairs grow from the fatty layer in your skin.

Your Nerve Endings in Action

So just how do your nerve endings help you feel things?

Touch the clothes you are wearing with your fingertips.

The nerve endings in your fingertips detect how the clothes feel.

Then they send this information as messages along pathways of nerve cells to your brain.

Some of your nerve endings detect **textures** such as rough and smooth. Others detect if things are hot or cold. Some nerve endings detect **pressure**, such as a tap on your arm. Many of your nerve endings detect pain.

When your brain receives the messages, you feel that the fabric is smooth, woolly, soft, or rough.

Jeans
Nerve endings
Epidermis

To your brain

This picture shows what happens when your fingertip touches your jeans.

1 The epidermis touches the fabric.

2 The nerve endings in the dermis detect rough jeans.

3 Messages are sent to your brain, and then you feel rough jeans.

OUCH!
That Hurts

Your sense of touch helps keep you safe by making you feel pain.

If you touch a hot dish, the nerve endings in your hand go into action.

In an instant, they send out messages that your hand is in danger.

The messages speed along pathways of nerve cells to your spinal cord and brain.

In a flash, your **spinal cord** sends a message to your hand to pull away.

At the same time, your brain makes you feel pain so you know to stop touching the dish.

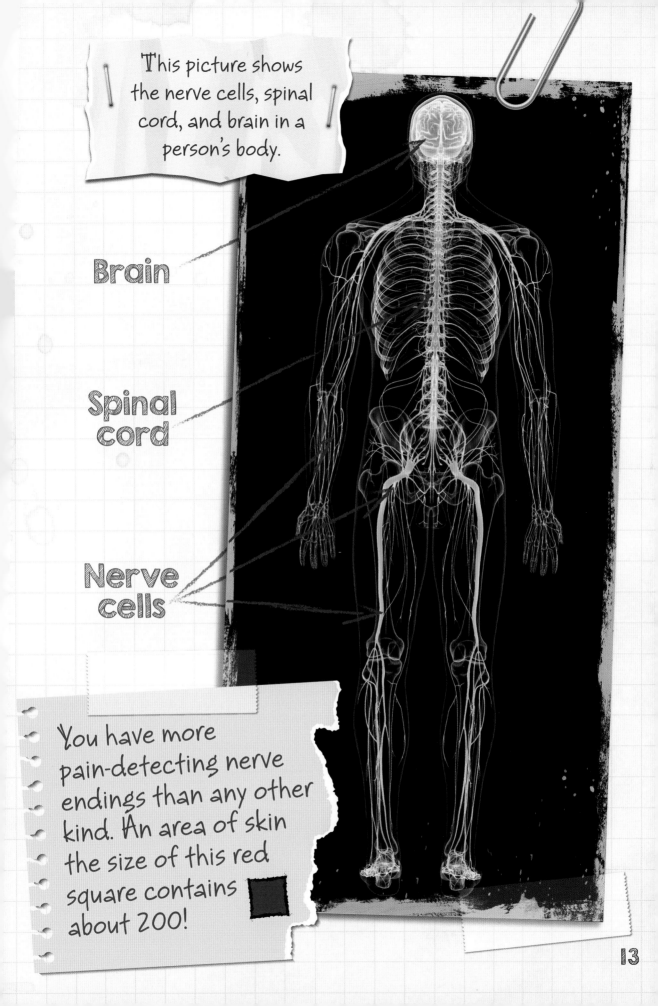

This picture shows the nerve cells, spinal cord, and brain in a person's body.

Brain

Spinal cord

Nerve cells

You have more pain-detecting nerve endings than any other kind. An area of skin the size of this red square contains about 200!

Scratch That Itch

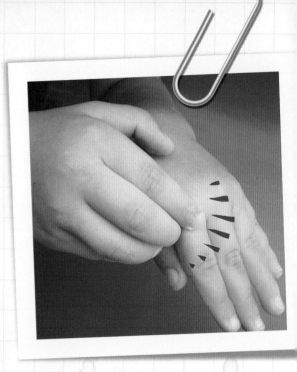

It's your sense of touch that allows you to feel annoying itches.

You often can't see what's making you itch.

It might be a speck of dust, a hair, or a little thread from your clothes

As you move, the object moves, too, and makes tiny movements and scratches on your skin.

Your very sensitive nerve endings send a message to your brain that something is touching your skin.

Your brain makes you feel an itch so you quickly scratch the spot and remove the pesky object.

14

Itching is one of the ways that your body protects itself. An itch is often just some dust or a hair, but it could be a biting insect. By making you itch and scratch, your body protects itself from tiny invaders.

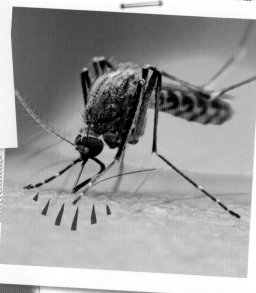

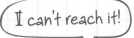

An itch that's hard to reach can drive you bananas!

Your Amazing Skin

Your skin is home to millions of nerve endings.

Some parts of your body are better at detecting touch than others.

This is because the skin in these places has more nerve endings.

Your fingertips and lips, for example, are very sensitive.

These body parts have many more nerve endings than your back or belly.

You have about 17,000 nerve endings on each of your hands!

Some blind people use their fingertips to read a type of writing called Braille. Instead of printed words, the words in a Braille book are made of tiny raised dots.

Braille writing

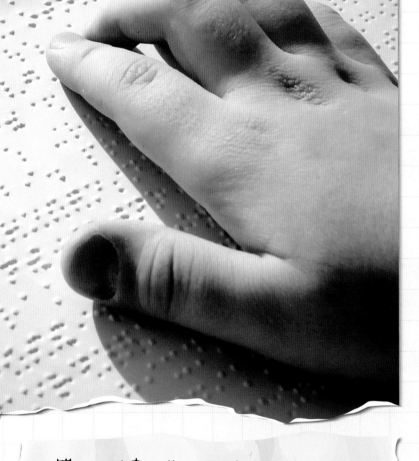

I read with my hands!

To read Braille, people gently touch the dots. Their fingertips are able to detect the different patterns of dots that make up the words.

Your Sensitive Tongue

It's not just the skin on the outside of your body that contains nerve endings.

Your tongue and the skin inside your mouth do, too.

When you lick ice cream, the nerve endings in your tongue detect that it's cold.

If you take a bite of something hot, the nerve endings in your mouth detect the heat.

They instantly send messages to your brain about the **temperature** of your food.

Being able to feel that food is hot helps stop you from burning your mouth.

The nerve endings on your tongue can feel the texture of your food. Feeling that your food is smooth, rough, hard, or soft makes eating more fun.

Sometimes you accidentally put food that's too hot into your mouth. Your nerve endings act fast by sending danger messages to your brain.

In less than a second, your brain makes you feel pain. This warns you that the food is hurting your tongue.

Your brain might even tell you to spit out the hot food!

I burned my tongue!

Care for Your Skin

Your hardworking skin protects your body and lets you feel the world around you.

It's important, therefore, that you take good care of it.

Every day, take a bath or shower and wash your skin with soap and water that's not too hot.

When you're out in the sun, always protect your skin by putting on sunscreen every two hours.

Remember! Look after your skin, and you'll be caring for your amazing sense of touch, too.

Sunscreen stops the sun's light from burning and hurting your skin. Always use a sunscreen that has an SPF, or sun protection factor, of 30 or higher.

When your skin is cut or scratched, a **scab** forms over the top of the **wound**. Under the protective scab, new skin cells grow to repair the cut.

Wound

Wash a cut or scratch with warm water and soap. You can also put a spray or cream on the wound that kills **germs**. Cover the wound with a bandage to keep it clean.

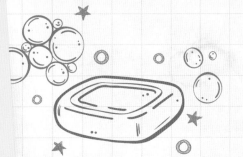

Glossary

cells (SELZ)
Very tiny parts of a living thing. Your bones, muscles, skin, hair, and every part of you are made of cells.

dermis (DUR-miss)
The middle layer of your skin that contains cells called nerve endings that detect touch.

detect (dee-TECT)
To recognize or identify something.

epidermis (ep-ih-DUR-miss)
The top and outside layer of your skin.

germs (JUHRMZ)
Tiny living things that are too small for you to see. Germs can harm your body or make you sick.

melanin (MEL-uh-nin)
A substance made by some of the cells in your epidermis that gives your skin its color.

microscope (MIKE-ruh-skope)
A tool or machine that is used to see things that are too small for people to see with their eyes alone.

nerve cells (NURV SELZ)
The billions of tiny cells that carry information back and forth between your brain and other parts of your body.

nerve endings (NURV EN-deengz)
Cells in the dermis layer of your skin that detect how things feel. Nerve endings can detect if something touching your skin is hot or cold. They can also detect texture, pressure, and pain.

pressure (PRESH-ur)
A force caused by touching, pressing, or squeezing something.

scab (SKAB)
A crust of dried blood that forms a protective covering over a cut or other wound.

sensations (sen-SAY-shuhnz)
Feelings that you detect with your sense of touch, such as hot, cold, or pain.

sense (SENSS)
One of the five ways that you collect information about the world around you. Your senses are seeing, hearing, smelling, tasting, and touching.

sensitive (SEN-sih-tiv)
Able to easily detect sensations, such as hot, cold, or pain.

spinal cord (SPY-nuhl KORD)
A long bundle of nerve cells that connects your brain with nearly every part of your body. Your spinal cord runs down your back and is protected by the bones of your spine.

temperature (TEMP-ruh-chur)
How hot or cold something is.

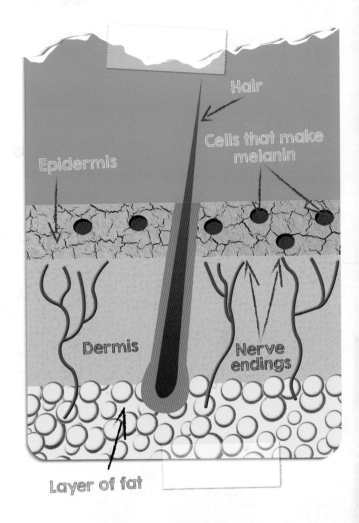

Hair

Cells that make melanin

Epidermis

Dermis

Nerve endings

Layer of fat

texture (TEX-chur)
How the surface of something feels. For example, an object might have a smooth or rough texture.

wound (WOOND)
A cut, scratch, or other injury that damages your skin.

Index

Read More

My Little Book about Me
Angela Royston
London: Quarto Library (2022).

A Journey Through the Human Body
Steve Parker
Beverly, MA: Quarto Library (2022).

Visit Us

www.SequoiaKidsMedia.com
Downloadable content and more!